THE LOVER OF GARDENS

THE LOVER OF GARDENS

COMPILED BY GAIL HARVEY

DESIGN BY LIZ TROVATO

GRAMERCY BOOKS

NEW YORK • AVENEL

Introduction and Compilation
Copyright © 1993 by Outlet Book Company, Inc.

This 1993 edition is published by Gramercy Books,
distributed by Outlet Book Company, Inc.
a Random House Company,
40 Engelhard Avenue
Avenel, New Jersey 07001

Random House
New York • Toronto • London • Sydney • Auckland

Printed and bound in the United States of America

Library of Congress Cataloging-in-Publication Data
The Lover of gardens.
p. cm.
ISBN 0-517-10022-3
1. Gardens—Literary collections. 2. English literature.
3. American literature.
PR1111.G3L68 1993
820'.8'036—-dc20   93-22849
                                                          CIP

8 7 6 5 4 3 2 1

INTRODUCTION

"A garden," wrote Francis Bacon, the seventeenth-century English philosopher and author, "is the purest of human pleasures. It is the greatest refreshment to the spirit...." Indeed, planting a garden is as creative as it is deeply satisfying, and watching a garden grow affirms and reaffirms the renewal of life.

But gardens have always been many things to men and women. They have been sites of pleasure and of pain, of refuge and danger. They have provided artists with inspiration and scientists with knowledge. They are places of real physical labor and soul-searching reflection. It is no wonder that so many writers through the ages have felt compelled to describe their own feelings about gardens.

This book is a collection of lovely insights, in prose and poetry, about gardens and gardening. Thomas Jefferson, for example, reflects that "no occupation is so delightful to me as the culture of the earth, and no culture comparable to that of the garden." Joseph Addison relates his philosophy of gardening and declares that "I look upon the pleasure which we take in a garden as one of the most innocent delights in human life" and Hanna Rion insists that "the greatest gift of the garden is the restoration of the five senses." Mrs. Francis King describes the bond between gardeners and, in his amusing poem "The Glory in the Garden," Rudyard Kipling reminds us "That half a proper gardener's work is done upon his knees."

Included, too, are charming excerpts from *The Secret Garden* by Frances Hodgson Burnett and *The Four Gardens* by "Handasyde," as well as poems by such great writers as Robert Browning, Percy Bysshe Shelley, Ralph Waldo Emerson, Christina Rossetti, Robert Louis Stevenson, and John Greenleaf Whittier.

Illustrated with paintings and drawings by Beatrice Parsons and Charles Robinson, which capture the essence of gardens, this book celebrates the beauty and the miracle of making something grow.

GAIL HARVEY

New York
1993

A garden should be in a constant state of fluid change, expansion, experiment, adventure; above all it should be an inquisitive, loving, but self-critical journey on the part of its owner.

H.E. BATES

To own a bit of ground, to scratch it with a hoe, to plant seeds and watch the renewal of life— this is the commonest delight of the race, the most satisfactory thing a man can do.

CHARLES DUDLEY WARNER

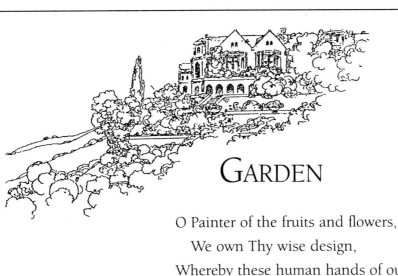

GARDEN

O Painter of the fruits and flowers,
    We own Thy wise design,
Whereby these human hands of ours
    May share the work of Thine!

Apart from Thee we plant in vain
    The root and sow the seed;
Thy early and Thy later rain,
    Thy sun and dew we need.

Our toil is sweet with thankfulness,
    Our burden is our boon;
The curse of Earth's gray morning is
    The blessing of its noon.

Why search the wide world everywhere
    For Eden's unknown ground?
That garden of the primal pair
    May nevermore be found.

But, blest by Thee, our patient toil
    May right the ancient wrong,
And give to every clime and soil
    The beauty lost so long.

Our homestead flowers and fruited trees
    May Eden's orchard shame;
We taste the tempting sweets of these
    Like Eve, without her blame.

And, north and south and east and west,
    The pride of every zone,
The fairest, rarest, and the best
    May all be made our own.

Its earliest shrines the young world sought
    In hill-groves and in bowers,
The fittest offerings thither brought
    Were Thy own fruits and flowers.

And still with reverent hands we cull
    Thy gifts each year renewed;
The good is always beautiful,
    The beautiful is good.

JOHN GREENLEAF WHITTIER

Who loves a garden still his

Eden keeps,

Perennial pleasures, plants, and

wholesome harvest reaps.

AMOS BRONSON ALCOTT

 I HAVE OFTEN THOUGHT THAT IF HEAVEN HAD given me choice of my position and calling, it should have been on a rich spot of earth, well watered, and near a good market for the productions of the garden. No occupation is so delightful to me as the culture of the earth, and no culture comparable to that of the garden. Such a variety of subjects, some one always coming to perfection, the failure of one thing repaired by the success of another, and instead of one harvest a continued one through the year. Under a total want of demand except for our family table, I am still devoted to the garden. But though an old man, I am but a young gardener.

THOMAS JEFFERSON

THE PLEASURE OF A GARDEN

I am one, you must know, who am looked upon as a humorist in gardening. I have several acres about my house, which I call my garden, and which a skillful gardener would not know what to call. It is a confusion of kitchen and parterre, orchard and flower garden, which lie so mixed and interwoven with one another, that if a foreigner, who had seen nothing of our country, should be conveyed into my garden at his first landing, he would look upon it as a natural wilderness, and one of the uncultivated parts of our country.

My flowers grow up in several parts of the garden in the greatest luxuriancy and profusion. I am so far from being fond of any particular one, by reason of its rarity, that if I meet with any one in a field which pleases me, I give it a place in my garden. By this means, when a stranger walks with me, he is surprised to see several large spots of ground covered with ten thousand different colors, and has often singled out flowers he might have met with under a common hedge, in a field, or in a meadow, as some of the greatest beauties of the place. The only method I observe in this particular is to range in the same quarter the products of the same season, that they may make their appearance together, and compose a picture of the greatest variety.

There is the same irregularity in my plantations, which run into as great a wilderness as their natures will permit. I take in none that do not naturally rejoice in the soil; and am pleased, when I am walking in a labyrinth of my own raising, not to know whether the next tree I shall meet with is an apple or oak, an elm or a pear tree.

My kitchen has likewise its particular quarters assigned it: for besides the wholesome luxury which that place abounds with, I have always thought a kitchen garden a more pleasant sight than the finest orangery, or artificial greenhouse. I love to see everything in its perfection: and am more pleased to survey my rows of coleworts and cabbages, with a thousand nameless potherbs, springing up in their full fragrancy and verdure, than to see the tender plants of foreign countries kept alive by artificial heats, or withering in an air and soil that are not adapted to them.

I must not omit that there is a fountain rising in the upper part of my garden, which forms a little wandering rill, and administers to the pleasure as well as the plenty of the place. I have so conducted it that it visits most of my plantations; and have taken particular care to let it run in the same manner as it would do in an open field, so that it generally passes through banks of violets and primroses, plats of willow or other plants, that seem to be of its own producing.

There is another circumstance in which I am very particular, or, as my neighbors call me, very whimsical; as my garden invites into it all the birds of the country, by offering them the conveniency of springs and shades, solitude and shelter, I do not suffer any one to destroy their nests in the spring, or drive them from their usual haunts in fruit-time. I value my garden more for being full of blackbirds than cherries, and very frankly give them fruit for their songs. By this means I have always the music of the season in its perfection, and am highly delighted to see the jay or the thrush hopping about my walks, and shooting before my eye across the several little glades and alleys that I pass through.

I think there are as many kinds of gardening as of poetry: your makers of parterres and flower gardens are epigrammatists and sonneteers in this art; contrivers of bowers and grottos, treillages and cascades, are romance writers.

As for myself, you will find, by the account which I have already given you, that my compositions in gardening are altogether after the Pindaric manner, and run into the beautiful wildness of nature, without affecting the nicer elegancies of art.

I have often wondered that those who are like myself, and love to live in gardens, have never thought of contriving a winter garden, which should consist of such trees only as never cast their leaves. We have very often little snatches of sunshine and fair weather in the most uncomfortable parts of the year, and have frequently several days in November and January that are as agreeable as any in the finest months. At such times, therefore, I think there could not be a greater pleasure than to walk in such a winter garden as I have proposed. In the summer season, the whole country blooms, and is a kind of garden; for which reason we are not so sensible of those beauties that at this time may be everywhere met with; but when Nature is in her desolation, and presents us with nothing but bleak and barren prospects, there is something unspeakably cheerful in a spot of ground which is covered with trees that smile amidst all the rigors of winter, and give us a view of the most gay season, in the midst of that which is most dead and melancholy. I have so far indulged myself in this thought, that I have set apart a whole acre of ground for the executing of it. The walls are covered with ivy instead of vines. The laurel, the hornbeam, and the holly, with many other trees and plants of the same nature, grow so thick in it that you cannot imagine a more lively scene. The glowing redness of the berries with which they are hung at this time vies with the verdure of their leaves. It is very pleasant, at the same time, to see the several kinds of birds retiring into this little green spot, and enjoying themselves among the branches and foliage, when my great garden does not afford a single leaf for their shelter.

I look upon the pleasure which we take in a garden as one of the most innocent delights in human life. A garden was the habitation of our first parents before the Fall. It is naturally apt to fill the mind with calmness and tranquillity, and to lay all its turbulent passions at rest. It gives us a great insight into the contrivance and wisdom of Providence, and suggests innumerable subjects for meditation. I cannot but think the very complacency and satisfaction which a man takes in these works of Nature to be a laudable if not a virtuous habit of mind.

JOSEPH ADDISON

God Almighty first planted
a garden.

FRANCIS BACON

The kiss of the sun for pardon,

　　The song of the birds for mirth;

One is nearer God's Heart in a garden

　　Than anywhere else on earth.

DOROTHY FRANCES GURNEY

MY
GARDEN

My garden is a pleasant place
Of sun glory and leaf grace.
There is an ancient cherry tree
Where yellow warblers sing to me,
And an old grape arbor, where
A robin builds her nest, and there
Above the lima beans and peas
She croons her little melodies,
Her blue eggs hidden in the green
Fastness of that leafy screen.
Here are striped zinnias that bees
Fly far to visit; and sweet peas,
Like little butterflies newborn,
And over by the tasseled corn
Are sunflowers and hollyhocks,
And pink and yellow four-o'clocks.
Here are hummingbirds that come
To seek the tall delphinium—
Songless bird and scentless flower
Communing in a golden hour.

There is no blue like the blue cup
The tall delphinium holds up,
Not sky, nor distant hill, nor sea,
Sapphire, nor lapis lazuli.

My lilac trees are old and tall;
I cannot reach their bloom at all.
They send their perfume over trees
And roofs and streets, to find the bees.

I wish some power would touch my ear
With magic touch, and make me hear
What all the blossoms say, and so
I might know what the winged things know.
I'd hear the sunflower's mellow pipe,
"Goldfinch, goldfinch, my seeds are ripe!"
I'd hear the pale wisteria sing,
"Moon moth, moon moth, I'm blossoming!"

I'd hear the evening primrose cry,
"Oh, firefly! come, firefly!"
And I would learn the jeweled word
The ruby-throated hummingbird
Drops into cups of larkspur blue,
And I would sing them all for you!

My garden is a pleasant place
Of moon glory and wind grace.
Of friend, whatever you may be,
Will you not come to visit me?
Over fields and streams and hills,
I'll pipe like yellow daffodils,
And every little wind that blows
Shall take my message as it goes.
A heart may travel very far
To come where its desires are,
Oh, may some power touch my ear,
And grant me grace, and make you hear!

Louise Driscoll

Verbal magic is the subtle mysterious power of certain words. This power may come from association with the senses; thus I have distinct sense of stimulation in the word scarlet, and pleasure in the words lucid and liquid. The word garden is a never ceasing delight; it seems to me oriental; perhaps I have a transmitted sense from my grandmother Eve of the Garden of Eden. I like the words, a Garden of Olives, a Garden of Herbs, the Garden of the Gods, a Garden enclosed, Philosophers of the Garden, the Garden of the Lord. As I have written on gardens, and thought on gardens, and walked in gardens, "the very music of the name has gone into my being." How beautiful are Cardinal Newman's words: "By a garden is meant mystically a place of spiritual repose, stillness, peace, refreshment, delight."

ALICE MORSE EARLE

WINIFRED CAVELY ROBINSON

garden is the purest of human pleasures. It is the greatest refreshment to the spirits of man, without which buildings and palaces are but gross handiworks.

FRANCIS BACON

THE GLORY OF THE GARDEN

Our England is a garden that is full of stately views,
Of borders, beds, and shrubberies and lawns and avenues,
With statues on the terraces and peacocks strutting by;
But the Glory of the Garden lies in more than meets the eye.

For where the old thick laurels grow, along the thin red wall,
You find the tool- and potting-sheds which are the heart of all;
The cold frames and the hothouses, the dungpits and the tanks,
The rollers, carts, and drainpipes, with the barrows and the planks.

And there you'll see the gardeners, the men and 'prentice boys
Told off to do as they are bid and do it without noise;
For, except when seeds are planted and we shout to scare the birds,
The Glory of the Garden it abideth not in words.

And some can pot begonias and some can bud a rose,
And some are hardly fit to trust with anything that grows;
But they can roll and trim the lawns and sift the sand and loam,
For the Glory of the Garden occupieth all who come.

Our England is a garden, and such gardens are not made
By singing,"Oh, how beautiful!" and sitting in the shade,
While better men than we go out and start their working lives
At grubbing weeds from gravel paths with broken dinner knives.

There's not a pair of legs so thin, there's not a head so thick,
There's not a hand so weak and white, not yet a heart so sick,
But it can find some needful job that's crying to be done,
For the Glory of the Garden glorifieth everyone.

Then seek your job with thankfulness and work till further orders,
If it's only netting strawberries or killing slugs on borders;
And when your back stops aching and your hands begin to harden,
You will find yourself a partner in the Glory of the Garden.

Oh, Adam was a gardener, and God who made him sees
That half a proper gardener's work is done upon his knees,
So when your work is finished, you can wash your hands and pray
For the Glory of the Garden, that it may not pass away!
And the Glory of the Garden it shall never pass away!

RUDYARD KIPLING

Earth laughs in flowers.

RALPH WALDO EMERSON

From THE SECRET GARDEN

It was the sweetest, most mysterious-looking place anyone could imagine. The high walls which shut it in were covered with the leafless stems of climbing roses which were so thick that they were matted together. Mary Lennox knew they were roses because she had seen a great many roses in India. All the ground was covered with grass of a wintry brown and out of it grew clumps of bushes which were surely rosebushes if they were alive. There were numbers of standard roses which had so spread their branches that they were like little trees. There were other trees in the garden, and one of the things which made the place look strangest and loveliest was that climbing roses had run all over them and swung down long tendrils which made light swaying curtains, and here and there they had caught at each other or at a far-reaching branch and had crept from one tree to another and made lovely bridges of themselves. There were neither leaves nor roses on them now and Mary did not know whether they were dead or alive, but their thin gray or brown branches and sprays looked like a sort of hazy mantle spreading over everything, walls, and trees, and even brown grass, where they had fallen from their fastenings and run along the ground. It was this hazy tangle from tree to tree which made it all look so mysterious. Mary had thought it must be different from other gardens which had not been left all by themselves so long, and indeed it was different from any other place she had ever seen in her life.

"How still it is!" she whispered. "How still!"

Then she waited a moment and listened at the stillness. The robin, who had flown to his treetop, was still as all the rest. He did not even flutter his wings; he sat without stirring, and looked at Mary.

"No wonder it is still," she whispered again. "I am the first person who has spoken in here for ten years."

She moved away from the door, stepping as softly as if she were afraid of awakening someone. She was glad that there was grass under her feet and that her steps made no sounds. She walked under one of the fairylike gray arches between the trees and looked up at the sprays and tendrils which formed them.

"I wonder if they are all quite dead," she said. "Is it all a quite dead garden? I wish it wasn't."

But she was *inside* the wonderful garden and she could come through the door under the ivy any time and she felt as if she had found a world all her own.

The sun was shining inside the four walls and the high arch of blue sky over this particular piece of Misselthwaite seemed even more brilliant and soft than it was over the moor. The robin flew down from his tree-top and hopped about or flew after her from one bush to another. He chirped a good deal and had a very busy air, as if he were showing her things. Everything was strange and silent and she seemed to be hundreds of miles away from anyone, but somehow she did not feel lonely at all. All that troubled her was her wish that she knew whether all the roses were dead, or if perhaps some of them had lived and might put out leaves and buds as the weather got warmer. She did not want it to be a quite dead garden. If it were a quite alive garden, how wonderful it would be, and what thousands of roses would grow on every side!

Her skipping-rope had hung over her arm when she came in and after she had walked about for a while she thought she would skip round the whole garden, stopping when she wanted to look at things. There seemed to have been grass paths here and there, and in one or two corners there were alcoves of evergreen with stone seats or tall moss-covered flower urns in them.

As she came near the second of these alcoves she stopped skipping.

There had once been a flowerbed in it, and she thought she saw something sticking out of the black earth—some sharp little pale-green points. She knelt down to look at them.

"Yes, they are tiny growing things and they *might* be crocuses or snowdrops or daffodils," she whispered.

She bent very close to them and sniffed the fresh scent of the damp earth. She liked it very much.

"Perhaps there are some other ones coming up in other places," she said. "I will go all over the garden and look."

She did not skip, but walked. She went slowly and kept her eyes on the ground. She looked in the old border beds and among the grass, and after she had gone round, trying to miss nothing, she had found ever so many more sharp, pale-green points, and she had become quite excited again.

"It isn't a quite dead garden," she cried out softly to herself. "Even if the roses are dead, there are other things alive."

She did not know anything about gardening, but the grass seemed so thick in some of the places where the green points were pushing their way through that she thought they did not seem to have room enough to grow. She searched about until she found a rather sharp piece of wood and knelt down and dug and weeded out the weeds and grass until she made nice little clear places around them.

"Now they look as if they could breathe," she said, after she had finished with the first ones. "I am going to do ever so many more. I'll do all I can see. If I haven't time today I can come tomorrow."

She went from place to place, and dug and weeded, and enjoyed herself so immensely that she was led on from bed to bed and into the grass under the trees. The exercise made her so warm that she first threw her coat off, and then her hat, and without knowing it she was smiling down on the grass and the pale-green points all the time. . . .

Mistress Mary worked in her garden until it was time to go to her midday dinner. In fact, she was rather late in remembering, and when she put on her coat and hat, and picked up her skipping-rope, she could not believe that she had been working two or three hours. She had been actually happy all the time; and dozens and dozens of the tiny, pale-green points were to be seen in cleared places, looking twice as cheerful as they had looked before when the grass and weeds had been smothering them.

"I shall come back this afternoon," she said, looking all round at her new kingdom, and speaking to the trees and the rosebushes as if they heard her.

Then she ran lightly across the grass, pushed open the slow old door, and slipped through it under the ivy.

FRANCES HODGSON BURNETT

On this June day the buds in my garden are almost as enchanting as the open flowers. Things in bud bring, in the heat of a June noontide, the recollection of the loveliest days of the year—those days of May when all is suggested, nothing yet fulfilled.

Mrs. Francis King

Flowers are the expression of God's love to man. One of the highest uses, therefore, which can be made in contemplating these beautiful creations, in all their variety and splendor, is that our thoughts and affections may be drawn upwards to Him who has so bountifully spread over the face of the whole earth such a vast profusion of these beautiful objects as tokens of His love to us. The more we examine flowers, especially when the eye is assisted by the microscope, the more we must adore the matchless skill of the Great Supreme. We must be ungrateful indeed, not to acknowledge His unspeakable goodness in thus providing so liberally for the happiness and pleasure of His children here below.

JOSEPH BECK

A COUNTRY PARSON'S GARDEN

This is Monday morning. It is a beautiful sunshiny morning early in July. I am sitting on the steps that lead to my door, somewhat tired of the duty of yesterday, but feeling very restful and thankful. Before me there is a little expanse of the brightest grass, too little to be called a lawn, very soft and mossy, and very carefully mown. It is shaded by three noble beeches, about two hundred years old. The sunshine around has a green tinge from the reflection of the leaves. Double hedges thick and tall, the inner one of gleaming beach, shut out all sight of a country lane that runs hard by; a lane into which this graveled sweep of would-be avenue enters, after winding deftly through evergreens rich and old, so as to make the most of its little length.

On the side farthest from the lane, the miniature lawn opens into a garden of no great extent, and beyond the garden you see a green field sloping upwards to a wood which bounds the view. One half of the front of the house is covered to the roof by a climbing rose tree, so rich now with cluster roses that you see only the white, soft masses of fragrance. Crimson roses and fuchsias cover halfway up the remainder of the front wall; and the sides of the flight of steps are green with ivy.

If ever there was a dwelling embosomed in great trees and evergreens it is here. Everything grows beautifully, oaks, horse chestnuts, beeches, laurels, yews, hollies, lilacs, and hawthorn trees. Off a little way on the right, graceful in stem, in branches, in the pale bark, in the light green leaves, I see my especial pet, a fair acacia.

This is the true country; not the poor shadow of it which you have near great and smoky towns. That sapphire air is polluted by no factory chimney. Smoke is a beauty here. There is a little of it, rising thin and blue from the cottage, hospitable and friendly looking from the rare mansion. The town is five miles distant; there is not even a village near. Green fields are all about; hawthorn hedges and rich hedge-rows, great masses of wood everywhere. But this is Scotland, and there is no lack of hills and rocks, of little streams and waterfalls; and two hundred yards off, winding round that churchyard, whose white stones you see by glimpses, through old oak branches, a large river glides a swiftly by. It is a quiet and beautiful scene, and it pleases me to think that Britain has thousands and thousands like it.

I have been sitting here for an hour, with a book on my knee, and upon that a piece of paper whereon I have been noting down some thoughts for the sermon which I hope to write during this week, and to preach next Sunday in that little parish church of which you can see a corner of a gable through the oaks which surround the churchyard.

A.K.H.B.

HER COTTAGE WAS SO SMOTHERED IN HER garden it was difficult to tell which was which, and every plant and flower had attained to its full growth. But the hedge was so thick it was impossible to see the garden at all without standing on the top step of the three little steps that led from the lane to the garden gate. The gate was painted greeny blue, so was the wooden bench, set for gossips close alongside the door. The cottage stood at right angles to the lane, with one small window in the gable looking directly into the apple tree. The path from the gate to the door was paved with flat red stones, scoured like everything about the cottage, and nearly as spotless as the snowy linen hanging on the hedge to dry.

The tub stood on a little trestle on the brick pathway beside the cottage door, and the woman who came to pick the syringa had her arms white with soapsuds to above the elbow. Tendrils and creepers and sprays of luxuriant plants laid hold of her lilac dress as she came along the path, while the crimson thorns of a great rosebush held her forcibly as she stood to chat by the gate. The rose was the deep damask, Rosa damascena, and the scent of its velvet petals sweeter than any spice of Ceylon. A border of white pinks had overgrown both the flowerbed and the edge of the path; there were columbines of a quaint celestial blue, roses, crimson, pink, and white; besides which there were bushes of Canterbury bells, the giant double variety, like pink and blue and silver cups set each in a saucer of its own. A stack of larkspur behind the damask rose put the columbines completely in the shade; there were stocks, too, and plots of sweet william more velvety and crimson than the rose.

"HANDASYDE"

THE GARDEN'S GIFT

The greatest gift of a garden is the restoration of the five senses.

During the first year in the country I noticed but few birds, the second year I saw a few more, but by the fourth year the air, the tree-tops, the thickets and ground seemed teeming with bird life. "Where did they all suddenly come from?" I asked myself. The birds had always been there, but I hadn't the power to see; I had been made purblind by the city and only gradually regained my power of sight.

My ears, deafened by the ceaseless whir and din of commerce, had lost the keenness which catches the nuances of bird melody, and it was long before I was aware of distinguishing the varying tones that afterward meant joy, sorrow, loss, or love to me. That hearing has now become so keen, there is no bond of sleep so strong that the note of a strange bird will not pierce to the unsleeping, subconscious ear and arouse me instantly to alertness in every fiber of my being. I wonder if even death will make me insensate to the first chirp of a vanguard robin in March.

During that half-awake first year of country life I was walking with a nature-wise man, and as we passed by a field where the cut hay lay wilting, he whiffed and said, "There's a good deal of ragweed in that hay." I gazed on him with the admiration I've saved all my life for wizards and wondered what peculiar brand of nose he had.

Then the heart, the poor jaded heart, that must etherize itself to endure the grimness of city life at all, how subtly it begins throbbing again in unison with the great symphony of the natural. The awakened heart can sense spring in the air when there is no visible suggestion in calendar or frosted earth, and knowing the songful secret, the heart can cause the feet to dance through a day that would only mean winter to an urbanite.

The sense of taste can only be restored by a constant diet of unwilted vegetables and freshly picked fruit.

The delicacy of touch comes back gradually by tending injured birdlings, by the handling of fragile infant plants, and by the acquaintance with different leaf textures, which finally makes one able to distinguish a plant, even in the dark, by its Irish-tweed, silken, or fur finish.

And the foot, how intangibly it becomes sensitized; how instinctively it avoids a plant even when the eye is busy elsewhere. On the darkest night I can traverse the rocky ravine, the thickets, the sinuous paths through overgrown patches, and never stumble, scratch myself, or crush a leaf. My foot knows every unevenness of each individual bit of garden, and adjusts itself lovingly without conscious thought of brain.

To the ears that have learned to catch the first tentative lute of a marsh frog in spring, orchestras are no longer necessary. To the eyes that have regained their sight, more wonder lies in the craftsmanship of a tiny leaf-form of inconsequential weed than is to be found in a bombastic arras. To the resuscitated nose is revealed the illimitable secrets of earth incense, the whole gamut of flower perfume, and other fragrant odors too intangible to be classed, odors which wing the spirit to realms our bodies are as yet too clumsy to inhabit.

To the awakened mind there is nothing so lowly in the things below and above ground but can command respect and study. Darwin spent only thirty years on the study of the humble earthworm.

To get the greatest good from a garden we should not undertake more than we can personally take care of. I have not had a gardener since the first year when outside help was necessary for the translation of the sumach and briar patches of our wilderness into arable land. A gardener is only helpful for the preliminary work of spading, after that his very presence is a profanation.

Garden making is creative work, just as much as painting or writing a poem. It is a personal expression of self, an individual conception of beauty. I should as soon think of asking a secretary to write my book, or the cook to assist in a watercolor painting, as to permit a gardener to plant or dig among my flowers.

HANNA RION

AFTER MANY GARDENS HAVE BEEN CONSIDERED, and their inhabitants have been located and scanned, it often seems that those in which the individuality of the owners had run riot were the ones to live longest in the memory. For the garden is not only a place in which to make things grow and to display the beautiful flowers of the earth, but a place that should accord with the various moods of its admirers. It should be a place in which to hold light banter, a place in which to laugh, and, besides, should have a hidden corner in which to weep. But above all, perhaps, it should be a place of sweet scent and sentiment.

A garden without the fragrance of flowers would be deprived of one of its true rights. Fortunately, those near the sea are unusually redolent of sweet scent, the soft moisture of the atmosphere that surrounds them causing their fragrance to be more readily perceived than if the atmosphere were harsh and dry. It is still an open question to what extent the memory and the imagination of people are stirred by scents recurring at intervals through their existence. To many the perfume of flowers has more meaning than their outward beauty. In it they feel the spirit and the eternity of the flowers.

Undoubtedly, a particular fragrance will bring back quickly to the mind, and with much vividness, scenes and associations which have apparently been forgotten and which might otherwise lie dormant for a lifetime. The odors of many flowers are very distinctive. The perfume of the strawberry shrub is like none other; fraxinella, lavender, lilacs, and an infinite number of flowers are as well known by their fragrance as by their appearance. And although we smell them a hundred times a season, under many and dissimilar circumstances, there is perhaps only the one association that they will definitely recall. It is the one that has affected us deeply and moved our sentiment.

The first strawberry shrub that I ever saw was given to me when a small child by a red-cheeked boy just as I went into church with my grandmother. I slipped it into the palm of my hand under my glove, and throughout the service I kept my nose closely to the opening of the glove, smelling the flower. I was reproved again and again, but I continually reverted to my new and exquisite diversion; for, in those days, the time spent in church seemed longer than the rest of the whole week. Even now, each spring, when the first of these strange little flowers gives its scent to the air, I am for an instant transplanted, as it were, back to that stiff church pew, aching to be out in the open, and smelling the strawberry shrub in my glove.

ALICE LOUNSBERRY

M en plant flowers because it represents a way of affirming the renewability of life—watching them grow each year, you know you can do it again next year.

AUTHOR UNKNOWN

From THE SENSITIVE PLANT

A Sensitive Plant in a garden grew,
And the young winds fed it with silver dew,
And it opened its fanlike leaves to the light,
And closed them beneath the kisses of night.

And the Spring arose on the garden fair,
Like the Spirit of Love felt everywhere;
And each flower and herb on Earth's dark breast
Rose from the dreams of its wintry rest.

But none ever trembled and panted with bliss
In the garden, the field, or the wilderness,
Like a doe in the noontide with love's sweet want,
As the companionless Sensitive Plant.

The snowdrop, and then the violet,
Arose from the ground with warm rain wet,
And their breath was mixed with fresh odor, sent
From the turf, like the voice and the instrument.

Then the pied windflowers and the tulip tall,
And narcissi, the fairest among them all,
Who gaze on their eyes in the stream's recess,
Till they die of their own dear loveliness;

And the naiadlike lily of the vale,
Whom youth makes so fair and passion so pale,
That the light of its tremulous bells is seen
Through their pavilions of tender green;

And the hyacinth purple, and white, and blue,
Which flung from its bells a sweet peal anew
Of music so delicate, soft, and intense,
It was felt like an odor within the sense;

And the rose like a nymph to the bath addrest,
Which unveiled the depth of her glowing breast,
Till, fold after fold, to the fainting air
The soul of her beauty and love lay bare:

And the wandlike lily, which lifted up,
As a maenad, its moonlight-colored cup,
Till the fiery star, which is its eye,
Gazed through clear dew on the tender sky;

And the jessamine faint, and the sweet tuberose,
The sweetest flower for scent that blows;
And all rare blossoms from every clime
Grew in that garden in perfect prime.

PERCY BYSSHE SHELLEY

My Mother's Garden

Her heart is like her garden,
Old-fashioned, quaint, and sweet,
With here a wealth of blossoms,
And there a still retreat.
Sweet violets are hiding,
We know as we pass by,
And lilies, pure as angel thoughts,
Are opening somewhere nigh.

Forget-me-nots there linger,
To full perfection brought,
And there bloom purple pansies
In many a tender thought.
There love's own roses blossom,
As from enchanted ground,
And lavish perfume exquisite
The whole glad year around.

And in that quiet garden—
The garden of her heart—
Songbirds are always singing
Their songs of cheer apart.

And from it floats forever,
O'ercoming sin and strife,
Sweet as the breath of roses blown,
The fragrance of her life.

ALICE E. ALLEN

He who plants a garden
plants happiness.

CHINESE PROVERB

THE FLOWER'S NAME

Here's the garden she walked across,
    Arm in my arm, such a short while since:
Hark, now I push its wicket, the moss
    Hinders the hinges and makes them wince!
She must have reached this shrub ere she turned,
    As back with that murmur the wicket swung;
For she laid the poor snail, my chance foot spurned,
    To feed and forget it the leaves among.

Down this side of the gravel walk
    She went while her robe's edge brushed the box:
And here she paused in her gracious talk
    To point me a moth on the milk-white flox.
Roses, ranged in a valiant row,
    I will never think that she passed you by!
She loves you noble roses, I know;
    But yonder, see, where the rock plants lie!

This flower she stopped at, finger on lip,
    Stooped over, in doubt, as settling its claim;
Till she gave me, with pride to make no slip,
    Its soft meandering Spanish name.
What a name! Was it love, or praise?
    Speech half-asleep, or song half-awake?
I must learn Spanish, one of these days,
    Only for that slow sweet name's sake.

Roses, if I live and do well,
    I may bring her, one of these days,
To fix you fast with as fine a spell,
    Fit you each with his Spanish phrase!
But do not detain me now; for she lingers
    There, like sunshine over the ground,
And ever I see her soft white fingers
    Searching after the bud she found.

Flower, you Spaniard, look that you grow not,
    Stay as you are and be loved forever!
Bud, if I kiss you 'tis that you blow not,
    Mind, the shut pink mouth opens never!
For while thus it pouts, her fingers wrestle,
    Twinkling the audacious leaves between,
Till round they turn and down they nestle—
    Is not the dear mark still to be seen?

Where I find her not, beauties vanish;
    Whither I follow her, beauties flee;
Is there no method to tell her in Spanish
    June's twice June since she breathed it with me?
Come, bud, show me the least of her traces,
    Treasure my lady's lightest footfall—
Ah, you may flout and turn up your faces—
    Roses, you are not so fair after all.

                                    ROBERT BROWNING

THE LOVE OF FLOWERS BRINGS SURELY WITH IT the love of all the green world. For love of flowers every blooming square in cottage gardens seen from the flying windows of the train has its true and touching message for the traveler; every bush and tree in nearer field and farther wood becomes an object of delight and stirs delightful thought. When I see a rhubarb plant in a small rural garden, I respect the man, or more generally the woman, who placed it there. If my eye lights upon the carefully tended peony held up by a barrel hoop, the round group of an old dicentra, the fine upstanding single plant of iris, at once I experience the warmest feeling of friendliness for that householder, and wish to know and talk with them about their flowers. For at the bottom there is a bond which breaks down every other difference between us. We are "Garden Souls."

MRS. FRANCIS KING

If you want to be happy for an hour,
roast a pig.
If you want to be happy for a year, marry.
If you want to be happy for a lifetime,
plant a garden.

CHINESE PROVERB

MY GARDEN

A garden is a lovesome thing, God wot!
Rose plot,
Fringed pool,
Ferned grot—
The veriest school
Of peace; and yet the fool
Contends that God is not—
Not God! in gardens! when the eve is cool?
Nay, but I have a sign;
'Tis very sure God walks in mine.

T. E. BROWN

My Garden

If I could put my words in song
    And tell what's there enjoyed,
All men would to my gardens throng,
    And leave the cities void.

In my plot no tulips blow,
    Snow-loving pines and oaks instead;
And rank the savage maples grow
    From Spring's faint flush to Autumn red.

My garden is a forest ledge
    Which older forests bound;
The banks slope down to the blue lake edge,
    The plunge to depths profound.

Here once the deluge plowed,
    Laid the terraces, one by one;
Ebbing later whence it flowed,
    They bleach and dry in the sun.

The sowers made haste to depart,
    The wind and the birds which sowed it;
Not for fame, nor by rules of art,
    Planted these, and tempests flowed it.

Waters that wash my garden side
    Play not in Nature's lawful web,
They heed not moon or solar tide,
    Five years elapse from flood to ebb.

Hither hasted in old time, Jove,
    And every god—none did refuse;
And be sure at last came Love,
    And after love, the Muse.

Keen ears can catch a syllable,
    As if one spake to another,
In the hemlocks tall, untamable,
    And what the whispering grasses smother

Æolian harps in the pine
    Ring with the song of the Fates;
Infant Bacchus in the vine
    Far distant yet his chorus waits.

Canst thou copy in verse one chime
    Of the wood-bell's peal and cry,
Write in a book the morning's prime,
    Or match with words that tender sky?

Wonderful verse of the gods,
    Of one import of varied tone;
They chant the bliss of their abodes
    To man imprisoned in his own.

Ever the words of the gods resound;
    But the porches of man's ear
Seldom in this low life's round
    Are unsealed, that he may hear.

Wandering voices in the air
    And murmurs in the wold
Speak what I cannot declare,
    Yet cannot all withhold.

When the shadow fell on the lake,
    The whirlwind in ripples wrote
Air-bells of fortune that shine and break,
    And omens above thought.

But the meanings cleave to the lake,
    Cannot be carried in book or urn;
Go thy ways now, come later back,
    On waves and hedges still they burn.

These the fates of men forecast,
    Of better men than live today;
If who can read them comes at last
    He will spell in the sculpture, "Stay."
            RALPH WALDO EMERSON

A GARDEN SONG

Here, in this sequestered close,
Bloom the hyacinth and rose;
Here, beside the modest stock,
Flaunts the flaring hollyhock;
Here, without a pang, one sees
Ranks, conditions, and degrees.

All the seasons run their race
In this quiet resting place;
Peach, and apricot, and fig
Here will ripen, and grow big
Here is store and overplus—
More had not Alcinous!

Here, in alleys cool and green,
Far ahead the thrush is seen;
Here, along the southern wall,
Keeps the bee his festival;
All is quiet else-afar
Sounds of toil and turmoil are.

Here be shadows large and long;
Here be spaces meet for song;
Grant, O garden-god, that I,
Now that mood and moment please,
Find the fair Pierides!

HENRY AUSTIN DOBSON

A GARDEN SONG

I scorn the doubts and cares that hurt
    The world and all its mockeries;
My only care is now to squirt
    The ferns among my rockeries.

In early youth and later life
    I've seen an up and seen a down,
And now I have a loving wife
    To help me peg verbena down.

Of joys that come to womankind
    The loom of fate doth weave her few,
But here are summer joys entwined
    And bound with golden feverfew.

I've learnt the lessons one and all
    With which the world its sermon stocks;
Now, heedless of a rise or fall,
    I've Brompton and I've German stocks.

In peace and quiet pass our days,
    With nought to vex our craniums;
Our middle beds are all ablaze
    With red and white geraniums.

Who Loves A Garden

Who loves a garden
Finds within his soul
Life's whole;
He hears the anthem of the soil
While ingrates toil;
And sees beyond his little sphere
The waving fronds of heaven, clear.

Louise Seymour Jones

NOTHING BUT OLD-FASHIONED FLOWERS GREW IN THE garden, and against the house all through the summer there was a delicate tangle of tendrils and flowers, pink roses and cherry pie, with a magnolia by the library windows and a giant jessamine on the garden side. In the border around their roots musk and verbena and sweet alyssum grew, till it almost seemed as though the garden were coming into the house by the ever open windows; for Lady Mary loved spicy breezes and liked to smell her flowers even when she lay in bed; the honeysuckle smelled all through the night, and evening primroses burnt like pale-yellow scented candles all about the garden. But roses were, after all, the beginning and end of Lady Mary's garden.

"HANDASYDE"

To A
Gardener

Friend, in my mountainside demesne
My plain-beholding, rosy, green,
And linnet-haunted garden-ground,
Let still the esculents abound.
Let first the onion flourish there,
Rose among roots, the maiden fair,
Wine-scented and poetic soul
Of the capacious salad bowl.

Let thyme the mountaineer—to dress
The tinier birds—and wading cress,
The lover of the shallow brook,
From all my plots and borders look.
Not crisp and ruddy radish, nor
Pease-cods for the child's pinafore

Be lacking; nor of salad clan
The last and least that ever ran
About great Nature's garden-beds.
Nor thence be missed the speary heads
Of artichoke; nor thence the bean
That gathered innocent and green
Outsavors the belauded pea.

These tend, I prithee; and for me,
Thy most long-suffering master, bring
In April, when the linnets sing
And the days lengthen more and more
At sundown to the garden door.
And I, being provided thus,
Shall, with superb asparagus,
A book, a taper, and a cup
Of country wine, divinely sup.

ROBERT LOUIS STEVENSON

He who knows what sweets and virtues are in the ground, the plants, the waters, the heavens, and how to come at these enchantments—is the rich and royal man.

RALPH WALDO EMERSON

SONNET

Written in a Country Retirement

Around my porch and lonely casement spread,
The myrtle never sere, and gadding vine,
With fragrant sweet-briar love to intertwine;
And in my garden's box-encircled bed
The pansy pied, and musk-rose white and red;
The pink, the lily chaste, and sweet woodbine,
Fling odors round; thick-woven eglantine
Decks my trim fence; in which, by silence led,
The wren hath wisely built her mossy cell,
Shelter'd from storms, in courtly land so rife,
And nestles o'er her young, and warbles well.
'Tis here with innocence in peaceful glen
I pass my blameless moments far from men,
Nor wishing death too soon, nor asking life.

JOHN CODRINGTON BAMPFYLDE

The Sundial

'Tis an old dial, dark with many a stain;
   In summer crowned with drifting orchard bloom,
Tricked in the autumn with the yellow rain,
   And white in winter like a marble tomb;

And round about its gray, time-eaten brow
   Lean letters speak—a worn and shattered row:
I am a Shade: a Shadowe too arte thou:
   I marke the Time: saye, Gossip, dost thou soe?

Here would the ringdoves linger, head to head;
   And here the snail a silver course would run,
Beating old Time; and here the peacock spread
   His gold-green glory, shutting out the sun.

HENRY AUSTIN DOBSON

HE SENT FOR THE GARDENER TO PULL UP ALL THE gay-colored blooms. He was mourning now, and nothing but purple flowers must henceforth grow in the garden they had both loved so well. Crocuses came early in the year; the bulbs had been sent from the Nottingham meadows, where crocuses grow wild. There were hepaticas and aubretia and beds of scented violets, large single violets almost as big as pansies, and Marie Louise, sweetest of Neapolitans, that begin to flower long before summer is past. Wisteria was trained against the low wall and long bunches of drooping mauve blossoms hung down thickly in rows from the straight symmetrical branches. Heliotrope also clambered up the wall, and a wreath of purple clematis hung like a heavy curtain against the old gray stones. There were lilac bushes at either end and pansies, long purples, ageratum, and stocks. A dark columbine, a purple larkspur, and some silvery mauve Canterbury bells. The lavender was a feature in itself; the plants had made so much wood and grown into small stocky shrubs. The soft gray foliage was always there, and made a background in the autumn for purple asters, great clumps of Michaelmas daisies, and a handsome show of chrysanthemums, shading from mauve to violet and purple and white. The garden was thus in complimentary mourning almost all the year round.

"HANDASYDE"

THE GARDEN IN SEPTEMBER

Now thin mists temper the slow-ripening beams
Of the September sun: his golden gleams
On gaudy flowers shine, that prank the rows
Of high-grown hollyhocks, and all tall shows
That Autumn flaunteth in his bushy bowers;
Where tomtits, hanging from the drooping heads
Of giant sunflowers, peck the nutty seeds;
And in the feathery aster bees on wing
Seize and set free the honied flowers,
Till thousand stars leap with their visiting:
While ever across the path mazily flit,
Unpiloted in the sun,
The dreamy butterflies
With dazzling colors powdered and soft glooms,
White, black, and crimson stripes, and peacock eyes,
Or on chance flowers sit,
With idle effort plundering one by one
The nectaries of deepest-throated blooms.

With gentle flaws the western breeze
Into the garden saileth,
Scarce here and there stirring the single trees,
For his sharpness he vaileth:
So long a comrade of the bearded corn,
Now from the stubbles whence the shocks are borne,

O'er dewy lawns he turns to stray,
As mindful of the kisses and soft play
Wherewith he enamored the light-hearted May,
Ere he deserted her;
Lover of fragrance, and too late repents;
Nor more of heavy hyacinth now may drink,
Nor spicy pink,
Nor summer's rose, nor garnered lavender,
But the few lingering scents
Of streakèd pea, and gillyflower, and stocks
Of courtly purple, and aromatic phlox.

And at all times to hear are drowsy tones
Of dizzy flies, and humming drones,
With sudden flap of pigeon wings in the sky,
Or the wild cry
Of thirsty rooks, that scour ascare
The distant blue, to watering as they fare
With creaking pinions, or—on business bent,
If aught their ancient polity displease—
Come gathering to their colony, and there
Settling in ragged parliament,
Some stormy council hold in the high trees.

ROBERT BRIDGES

An October Garden

In my autumn garden I was fain
   To mourn among my scattered roses;
   Alas for that last rosebud that uncloses
To Autumn's languid sun and rain
When all the world is on the wane!
   Which has not felt the sweet constraint of June,
   Nor heard the nightingale in tune.

Broad-faced asters by my garden walk,
   You are but coarse compared with roses:
   More choice, more dear that rosebud which uncloses,
Faint-scented, pinched, upon its stalk,
That least and last which cold winds balk;
   A rose it is though least and last of all,
   A rose to me though at the fall.

CHRISTINA ROSSETTI

THE GARDENER

The gardener does not love to talk,
He makes me keep the gravel walk;
And when he puts his tools away,
He locks the door and takes the key.

Away behind the currant row
Where no one else but cook may go,
Far in the plots, I see him dig
Old and serious, brown and big.

He digs the flowers, green, red, and blue,
Nor wishes to be spoken to.
He digs the flowers and cuts the hay,
And never seems to want to play.

Silly gardener! summer goes,
And winter comes with pinching toes,
When in the garden bare and brown
You must lay your barrow down.

Well now, and while the summer stays
To profit by these garden days
O how much wiser you would be
To play at Indian wars with me!

ROBERT LOUIS STEVENSON

L ast night, there came a frost, which has done great damage to my garden....It is sad that Nature will play such tricks with us poor mortals, inviting us with sunny smiles to confide in her, and then, when we are entirely within her power, striking us to the heart.

NATHANIEL HAWTHORNE

The garden that is
finished is dead.

H. E. BATES